LOTSA Luckovich

12/03

From the Pulitzer Prize Winning Editorial Cartoonist Mike Luckovich
with an introduction by Al Franken

LOTSA Luckovich

POCKET BOOKS

New York   London   Toronto   Sydney   Tokyo   Singapore

An *Original* Publication of POCKET BOOKS

POCKET BOOKS, a division of Simon & Schuster Inc.
1230 Avenue of the Americas, New York, NY 10020

Copyright © 1996 by Mike Luckovich
Introduction copyright © 1996 by Al Franken

All rights reserved, including the right to reproduce
this book or portions thereof in any form whatsoever.
For information address Pocket Books, 1230 Avenue
of the Americas, New York, NY 10020

ISBN: 0-671-54519-1

First Pocket Books trade paperback printing October 1996

10 9 8 7 6 5 4 3 2 1

POCKET and colophon are registered trademarks of
Simon & Schuster Inc.

Cover design by Mike Luckovich

Printed in the U.S.A.

To Margo, John, Mickey, and Micaela

Introduction
by Al Franken

I live in New York. And New York has only one decent daily newspaper, the *Times*. I'm not a fan of the *Daily News,* and the *New York Post* is, basically, a big stinking piece of trash. The only problem is that the *Times* doesn't allow cartoons. It's too classy for cartoons. Even editorial cartoons. Except on Sundays.

On Sundays, "The Week in Review" section features a small collection of that week's best editorial cartoons from around the nation. Invariably, this is the first part of the Sunday paper I turn to. Very often it's the most enjoyable ninety seconds of my week.

And that's usually because of a Mike Luckovich cartoon. He's there a lot. Because he's incredibly consistent. More than that, he's really funny. Also mean. Sometimes. Though never gratuitously.

One of my favorites came in the wake of the Susan Smith double murders in South Carolina. You'll remember she had police looking for "the black guy" who had "kidnapped" her boys. Luckovich's cartoon had Goldilocks explaining to Mama, Papa, and Baby Bear that "the black guy" had eaten their porridge.

But what I especially like about Luckovich is that he clearly doesn't like Newt Gingrich. And as the cartoonist for the Atlanta *Constitution,* he's proved that many times. "I love doing cartoons about Newt," Luckovich says, "because he's so thin-skinned." Something I know only too well.

In fact, this spring, after the White House Correspondents Dinner, Newt threatened to punch me in the nose. I knew he wouldn't, because he's not man enough. See, a man doesn't come to his wife's hospital room after her third cancer surgery and give her his terms for a divorce. Newt did this—and has acknowledged that he did—with his two daughters in tow.

And that sordid little episode provided the context for Luckovich's most famous cartoon: Newt visits the hospital room of a sick woman hooked to an I.V. She's labelled "Georgia Constituents." With his arms around two floozies clearly labelled "D.C. Highrollers," a smiling Newt tells the sick woman, "I want a divorce."

The cartoon ran the day before the 1994 election. Newt was so pissed off, he banned the *Constitution* from covering him. Like a true man, Newt justified his snit by hiding behind his children, saying that the cartoon depicted his daughters as hookers. A bit of a stretch. But to be fair, I'd be a little defensive about my daughters if I had abandoned them and failed to pay their child support. Newt did that too.

Don't hate Mike for the last three paragraphs. As I said, he can be mean, but never gratuitously. Myself? I think gratuitous meanness can be an effective and legitimate artistic tool.

MOMENT OF SILENT PRAYER AT BEGINNING OF CLASS.

O.J. UPDATE

WEEEE!

Videotape surfaces showing healthy O.J. playfully tossing Al Cowlings in air on day of murders.

The prosecution intends to call a meowing cat to corroborate the barking dog.

LATEST POLL

59% - THINK JUDGE ITO'S DOING A GOOD JOB.
27% - THINK HE'S DOING A POOR JOB.
14% - THINK HE'S GUILTY.

Defense to try to show police contaminated evidence by holding a square dance at crime scene.

O.J. to release book of poetry -

I WANT TO TELL YOU A LIMERICK
By O.J.

IF JEFFREY DAHMER HAD BEEN A FOOTBALL HERO.

ROSS PEROT CONTEMPLATES ANOTHER RUN

LARRY KING SHOW

AIN'T SAYIN' I WILL. AIN'T SAYIN' I WON'T. AIN'T SAYIN' I DO. AIN'T SAYIN' I DON'T. AIN'T SAYIN' I SUE. AIN'T SAYIN' I SONT. AIN'T SAYIN' I BLUE. AIN'T SAYIN' I BLONT....

HE'S COMING UP WITH FOLKSY NEW ANALOGIES—

THE DEFICIT'S LIKE A ZIT ON CLAUDIA SCHIFFER'S RUMP!..

HE'S PREPARING NEW CHARTS.

GIMME 13,573 CHARTS WITH THE ARROW GOIN' UP. AND 11,952 WITH THE ARROW GOIN' DOWN!...

HE'S THE KIND OF CANDIDATE FOLKS ARE HUNGRY FER.

DOLE AND CLINTON DON'T EXCITE ME. I WISH AN INSANE GNOME WERE RUNNING...

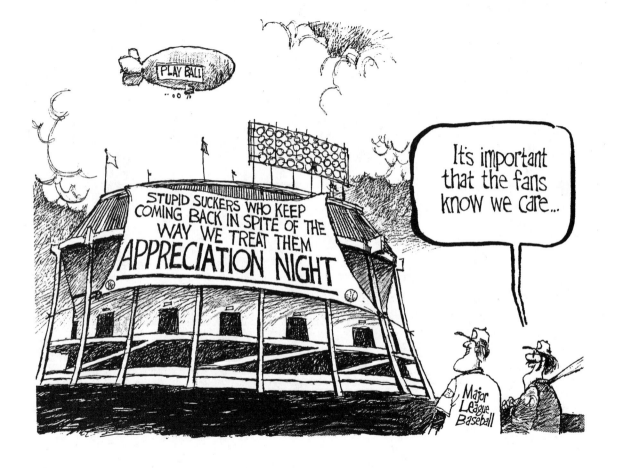

Dear Editor,
Please run "The Family Circus" real big on the front page.

Sincerely,
The Unabomber

The Washington Post

THE FAMILY CIRCUS

NEWS

THE FDA WANTS
TO TAKE HIS
CIGARETTES.
Don't Let Them

(PAID FOR BY THE TOBACCO INDUSTRY)

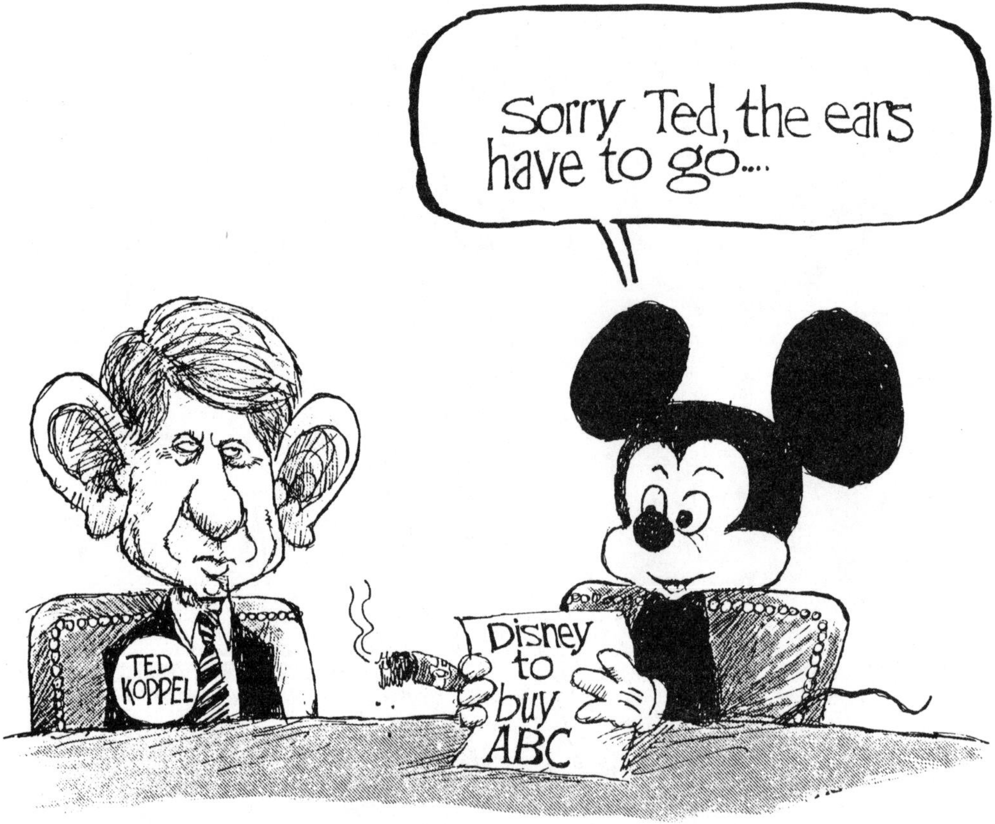
Sorry Ted, the ears have to go....
TED KOPPEL
Disney to buy ABC

Thanksgiving at the Bobbitts

STAR TREK- THE G.O.P. GENERATION

Rodin sculpture updated

BOB DOLE, AGE 1½